IT WORKS

Join the millions of readers who discovered . . .

THE FAMOUS LITTLE RED BOOK THAT MAKES YOUR DREAMS COME TRUE!

IT WORKS

A CLEAR, DEFINITE, COMMON-SENSE PLAN of ACCOMPLISHMENT

BY **R.H.J.**

Introduction by **MITCH HOROWITZ**

Published by Gildan Media LLC
aka G&D Media.
www.GandDmedia.com

It Works was originally published in 1926. Introduction © 2022 by Mitch Horowitz.

G&D Media edition 2022.

Cover design by Tom McKeveny

Interior design by Meghan Day Healey of Story Horse, LLC.

ISBN: 978-1-7225-0566-0

Introduction

The Three-Step Miracle

How a little red pamphlet changed the world—and may change you

By Mitch Horowitz

Can thoughts make things happen?

A middle-aged Chicagoan who beat the Great Depression believed so—and he anonymously spread his mind-power secret to the world. His beguiling method may hold special relevance for people struggling with the same issues today.

It Works

A SIMPLE IDEA

The messenger of success concealed his identity behind the initials R.H.J., which stood for Roy Herbert Jarrett. By profession, Jarrett was a salesman of typewriters and of printing machines. But the seeker-salesman accomplished what few ministers or practical philosophers ever could: He worked out an ethical philosophy of personal attainment, and couched it in everyday, immensely persuasive language. At age fifty-two, Jarrett brought his message to the world with a self-published, pocket-sized pamphlet called simply: *It Works*.

Published in 1926, Jarrett's concise pamphlet has never gone out of print. It has sold more than 1.5 million copies and remains popular—for good reason.

It Works

It Works is one of the most intriguing and infectious books ever written on mental manifestation. Anyone who wants to taste (or test) such ideas can finish Jarrett's pamphlet during a lunch break. And many people did so.

Wage-earning Americans who had never before given much thought to metaphysics wound up buying and often giving away large numbers of *It Works*, sending grateful testimonials to the address that Jarrett printed inside.

As the legend goes at the front of the booklet, Jarrett had sent his short manuscript to a friend for critique. Jarrett identified the friend only by the initials "J.F.S." The helper returned it with the notation: "IT WORKS," which Jarrett decided to use as his title.

It Works

The legend is true. The friend was Jewell F. Stevens, owner of an eponymous Chicago advertising agency, which specialized in religious items and books. In 1931, the advertising executive Stevens hired Jarrett to join his agency as a merchandising consultant and account manager. For Jarrett, the new position was deliverance from a tough, working-class background, and years of toil in the Willy Loman-domain of sales work. Jarrett became the example of his own success philosophy.

SALESMAN AND SEEKER

Roy Herbert Jarrett was born in 1874 to a Scottish immigrant household in Quincy, Illinois. His father worked as an iceman and a night watchman.

It Works

Roy's mother died when he was eight. By his mid-twenties, Roy was married and living in Rochester, New York, working as a sales manager for the Smith Premier Typewriter Company. His first marriage failed, and by 1905 he returned to the Midwest to marry a new wife and live closer to his aged father. In Chicago, Jarrett found work as a salesman for the American Multigraph Sales Company. It was the pivotal move of his life.

American Multigraph manufactured typewriters and workplace printing machinery. In a sense, the printing company was the Apple Computer of its day. The company's flagship product, the Multigraph, was an innovative, compact printing press. It took up no more space than an office desk and could be operated without specialized knowledge. The Multigraph was the first generation of easy-to-use printing devices, allowing offices to produce their own flyers, mailers, and newsletters. Its manufacturer possessed a sense of mission. American Multigraph had a reputation in the printing trade for its gung-ho culture and pep-rally sales conventions.

"For years," wrote the industry journal Office Appliances in September 1922, "a feature of every convention has been an address on 'The Romance of the Multigraph' by Advertising Manager Tim Thrift." On the surface, Thrift told his sales crew, the Multigraph could print labels, newsletters, and pamphlets—but one must peer into

It Works

"the soul of what to some appears as a machine." The Multigraph, he said, was "not a thing of metal, wood and paint; a mere machine sold to some man who can be convinced he should buy it. Ah, no! The Multigraph is a thing of service to the world . . ."

Cynics could laugh all they wanted, but for Jarrett the company's motivational tone, combined with the magical-seeming efficiency of modern printing, helped launch him on the idea of *It Works*.

"DAY BY DAY"

Jarrett's belief in inspirational business messages dovetailed with his interest in autosuggestion and mental conditioning. Such ideas reached Jarrett through the work of a French pharmacist and self-taught psychologist named Emile Coué, who had visited Chicago. Jarrett's vision grew from a cross-pollination of American business motivation and the ideals of the French mind theorist.

Born in Brittany in 1857, Coué developed an early interest in hypnotism, which he pursued through a mail-order course from Rochester, New York. Coué more rigorously studied hypnotic methods in the late 1880s with physician Ambroise-Auguste Liébeault. The French therapist Liébault was one of the founders of the so-called Nancy School of hypnotism, which promoted hypnotism's therapeutic uses.

While working as a pharmacist at Troyes in northwestern France in the

It Works

early 1900s, Coué made a startling discovery: Patients responded better to medications when he spoke in praise of the formula. Coué came to believe that the imagination aided not only in recovery but also in a person's general sense of well-being. From this insight, Coué developed a method of "conscious autosuggestion." It was a form of waking hypnosis that involved repeating confidence-building mantras while in a relaxed or semiconscious state.

Coué argued that many people suffer from poor self-image. Our willpower, or drive to achieve, he said, is constantly overcome by our imagination, by which he meant a person's unconscious self-perceptions.

It Works

"When the will and the imagination are opposed to each other," he wrote, "it is always the imagination which wins . . ." By way of example, he asked people to think of walking across a wooden plank laid on the floor — obviously an easy task. But if the same plank is elevated high off the ground, the task becomes fraught with fear even though the physical demand is the same. This, Coué asserted, is what we are constantly doing on a mental level when we imagine ourselves as worthless or weak.

Coué's method of autosuggestion was simplicity itself. He told patients to repeat the confidence-building mantra: *Day by day, in every way, I am getting better and better.*

It Works

It was to be recited twenty times each morning and evening, just loud enough to hear, while lying in bed upon awakening and before going to sleep, with eyes closed and the mind focused on what you desire. He advised using a string with twenty knots to count off the repetitions, as if counting rosary beads.

THE MAGIC HAND?

In the early 1920s, news of Coué's method reached America. The "Miracle Man of France" briefly grew into an international sensation. American newspapers featured Ripley's-Believe-It-Or-Not-styled drawings of Coué, looking like a goateed magician and gently displaying his knotted string at eye level like a hypnotic device. In early 1923, Coué made a three-week lecture tour of America. One of his final stops in February was in Jarrett's hometown, where the Frenchman delivered a talk at Chicago's Orchestra Hall.

In a raucous scene, a crowd of more than two thousand demanded that the therapist help a paralytic man who had been seated onstage. Coué defiantly told the audience that his autosuggestive treatments could work only on illnesses that originated in the mind. "I have not the magic hand!" he insisted. Nonetheless, Coué approached the man and told him to concentrate on his legs and to repeat, "It is passing, it is passing." The seated man struggled up and haltingly walked. The crowd exploded. Coué rejected any notion that his "cure" was miraculous and insisted that the man's disease must have been psychosomatic.

To some American listeners, Coué's message of self-affirmation held special relevance for oppressed people. The pages of black-nationalist Marcus Garvey's newspaper *Negro World* echoed Coué's day-by-day mantra in an editorial headline: "Every Day in Every Way We See Drawing Nearer and Nearer the Coming of the Dawn for Black Men." The paper editorialized that Marcus Garvey's teachings provided the same "uplifting psychic influence" as Coué's.

Coué took a special liking to Americans. He found American attitudes a refreshing departure from

It Works

what he knew back home. "The French mind," he wrote, "prefers first to discuss and argue on the fundamentals of a principle before inquiring into its practical adaptability to every-day life. The American mind, on the contrary, immediately sees the possibilities of it, and seeks . . . to carry the idea further even than the author of it may have conceived."

The therapist could have been describing the salesman-seeker Roy Jarrett. "A short while ago," Jarrett wrote in 1926, the year of Coué's death, "Dr. Emile Coué came to this country and showed thousands of people how to help themselves. Thousands of others spoofed at the idea, refused his assistance and are today where they were before his visit." But Jarrett saw the potential.

THREE-STEP MIRACLE

Taking his cue from the ease of Coué's approach, Jarrett devised "Three Positive Rules of Accomplishment" in *It Works*. In summary, they are:

1. *Carefully write a list of what you really want in life. Take as long as you need to get it right.*
2. *Once you are satisfied with your list, read it three times daily: morning, noon, and night. Think about what you want as often as possible.*
3. *Keep your practice and desires strictly to yourself. (This was intended to prevent other people's negative reactions from sullying your inner resolve.)*

It Works

Then, express silent gratitude each time an item on your list reaches you.

Just as Coué had observed about American audiences, Jarrett boldly expanded on the uses of autosuggestion. In the steps of the American metaphysical tradition, Jarrett believed that subconscious-mind training did more than recondition the mind: it activated a divine inner power that served to out-picture a person's mental images into the surrounding world. "I call this power 'Emmanuel' (God in us)," Jarrett wrote.

With its ease of methods, the self-published pamphlet quickly found an audience and ran through multiple printings. Many readers swore by it, and wrote in for additional copies to give away to friends (something Jarrett encouraged with a bulk-order form).

THAT'S IT?

It is tempting to look at Jarrett's three steps and ask: that's it? What reasonable person could believe, much less attempt, such a rudimentary, even childish, method to achievement?

Indeed, most detractors didn't try it—and never came to understand why the little book became one of the most popular, if below-the-radar, works of spiritual self-help.

The "secret" to *It Works* is that it compels us to do something we think that we do all the time but, in actuality, rarely try: come to terms with what we really want. We certainly believe that we know what we want. We constantly tell ourselves I'd like to buy that, work there, date him, and so on. But we rarely, if ever, sit down in a sustained and self-revealing way, stripped of all conformities and prejudices, and lay bare our truest, most absolute desires.

We may or may not want to act on those desires—there may be costs and burdens, ethical or otherwise. There may be unforeseen consequences or compromises. But just as often, we harbor within us a true, noble, and altogether sound life direction that we never articulate or attempt. This is because we are continually distracted by rote thought and internalized peer pressure. We almost never stop—completely stop—to ask: What do I really want?

It Works

And there may be more to the "simple" formula in this little book than just that. The clarified, motivated mind may also possess an agency that we have not yet fully reckoned with in modern Western life, but that is indicated in placebo studies, neuroplasticity, quantum enigmas, and psychical research. There may be unacknowledged mental properties and possibilities that this three-step program sets in motion, or at least hints at.*

NEW TESTAMENT

Jarrett's work broke through—but he felt incomplete. It wasn't that he chafed at using mind-power for material ends. Indeed, he urged readers to

---

* I explore these questions more fully in *One Simple Idea* and *The Miracle Club*.

It Works

use the book for money, possessions, or just about anything they wanted. But he believed that many had missed the book's deeper point. "Merely giving you the simple rules to accomplishment, with brief instructions as to their use," he wrote several years later, "while beneficial, is not satisfying."

Jarrett's deeper purpose in *It Works* was only hinted at by a mysterious symbol he placed on its cover. Below the title *It Works* appeared a simple drawing of a cross, with its bottom bent at a right angle. The square-and-cross appeared on every copy of the little red book until 1992, when a later publisher removed it. That symbol, wrote Jarrett's friend Stevens, "was really the undisclosed reason for the book."

It Works

What was this beguiling square-and-cross, which some readers ignored, some wondered at, and a publisher later cut?

Five years after producing *It Works*, Roy Jarrett made a little-known and final foray into publishing. In 1931, he produced a thoughtful and ambitious work, *The Meaning of the Mark*. The longer volume served as an inner key to *It Works*—it explained his strange symbol and dealt directly with the moral quandaries of success-based spirituality.

Jarrett explained that the cross-and-square was his personal symbol of spiritual awakening. Its meaning, he hoped, would be intuitively felt by readers. The square represented earthly values, particularly the need to treat others with the respect one seeks for oneself, which Jarrett saw as the hidden key to achievement. But there was another part to the matter. Personal attainment could find its lasting and proper purpose only when conjoined to the cross, the presence of God. Together, individual striving and receptivity to the Divine would bring man into the fullness of life. Jarrett wrote:

> *The definition of correct thinking for our purpose is: "thoughts which are harmoniously agreeable to God and man as a whole." Thoughts agreeable to God come to you through the intuitive messages from your soul, often inten-*

It Works

sified by the senses. Thoughts agreeable to man come to you more frequently through the senses and are often intensified by intuition.

By dwelling on the meaning of the square-and-cross, he reasoned, the reader could be constantly reminded to unite the two currents of life.

CALIFORNIA IDYLL

The success of *It Works* helped Jarrett attain a lifestyle that, while not extravagant, went beyond anything his laborer father could have hoped for. Jarrett and his wife retired to a sunny hacienda-style bungalow in a tidy middle-class section of Beverly

It Works

Hills. But their California idyll was fated to be short-lived. Jarrett died there in 1937 at age sixty-three of leukemia. He had been diagnosed three years earlier.

Jarrett didn't embark on his career as a writer until the final years of his life. He produced both of his books while in his fifties. His success arose not despite the lateness of his start but because of it. Like British seeker James Allen and the best New Thought pioneers, this self-educated man from ordinary life devised a philosophy that had been tested by the nature of his own personal conduct and lived experience. Only then did he deem it worth sharing.

It Works

THIS BOOK

WITH ITS VALUABLE MESSAGE

IS PRESENTED TO YOU

BY

....

It Works

All who joy would win must share it,
Happiness was born a twin.

—BYRON

Send "It Works" to *Your* Friends

To RHJ

*It Works**

JFS

* The author sent the manuscript of this book for criticism to a friend who returned it with the notation, "It Works." This judgment born of experience was adopted as the title of the book.—*Publishers*

A concise, definite, resultful plan with rules, explanations and suggestions for bettering your condition in life.

If you KNOW what you WANT you can HAVE IT

The man who wrote this book is highly successful and widely known for his generosity and helpful spirit. He gives full credit for all that he has accomplished in mastering circumstances, accumulating wealth and winning friends to the silent working out of the simple, powerful truth which he tells of in his work. He shows you here an easy, open road to a larger, happier life. Knowing that the greatest good comes from helping others without expecting praise, the author of this work has requested that his name be omitted.

What is the real secret of
obtaining desirable possessions?

*A*RE some people born under a lucky star or other charm which enables them to have all that which seems so desirable, and if not, what is the cause of the difference in conditions under which men live?

Many years ago, feeling that there must be a logical answer to this question, I decided to find out, if possible, what it was. I found the answer to my own satisfaction, and for years, have given the information to others who have used it successfully.

From a scientific, psychological or theological viewpoint, some of the following statements may be interpreted as incorrect, but nevertheless, the plan has brought the results desired to those who have followed the simple instructions, and it is my sincere belief that I am now presenting it in a way which will bring happiness and possessions to many more.

"IF wishes were horses, beggars would ride," is the attitude taken by the average man and woman in regard to possessions. They are not aware of a power so near that it is overlooked; so simple in operation that it is difficult to conceive; and so sure in results that it is not made use of consciously, or recognized as *the cause of failure or success.*

It Works

"GEE, I wish that were mine," is the outburst of Jimmy, the office boy, as a new red roadster goes by; and Florence, the telephone operator, expresses the same thought regarding a ring in the jeweler's window; while poor old Jones, the bookkeeper, during the Sunday stroll, replies to his wife, "Yes, dear, it would be nice to have a home like that, but it is out of the question. We will have to continue to rent." Landem, the salesman, protests that he does all the work, gets the short end of the money and will some day quit his job and find a real one, and President Bondum, in his private sanctorum, voices a bitter tirade against the annual attack of hay-fever.

It Works

At home it is much the same. Last evening, father declared that daughter Mabel was headed straight for disaster, and today, mother's allowance problem and other trying affairs fade into insignificance as she exclaims, "This is the last straw. Robert's school teacher wants to see me this afternoon. His reports are terrible, I know, but I'm late for Bridge now. She'll have to wait until tomorrow." So goes the endless stream of expressions like these from millions of people in all classes who give no thought to what they really want, *and who are getting all they are entitled to or expect.*

If you are one of these millions of thoughtless talkers or wishers and would like a decided change from your present condition, you can have it; but first of all you must *know what you want* and this is no easy task. When you can train your *objective mind* (the mind you use every day) to decide definitely upon the things or conditions you desire, you will have taken your first big step in accomplishing or securing what you know you want.

To get what you want is no more mysterious or uncertain than the radio waves all around you. Tune in correctly and you get a perfect result, but to do this, it is, of course, necessary to know something of your equipment and have a plan of operation. You have within you a *mighty power*, anxious and willing to serve you, a *power capable* of giving you *that which you earnestly desire*. This power is described by Thomson Jay Hudson, Ph.D., LL.D., author of "The Law of Psychic Phenomena," as your *subjective mind*. Other learned writers use different names and terms, *but all agree that it is omnipotent*. Therefore, I call this Power "Emmanuel" (God in us).

Regardless of the name of this Great Power, or the conscious admission of a God, the Power is *capable and willing* to carry to a complete and perfect conclusion every earnest desire of your objective mind, but you must be really in earnest about what you want. Occasional wishing or half-hearted wanting does not form a perfect connection or communication with *your omnipotent power.* You must be in earnest, *sincerely* and *truthfully* desiring certain conditions or things—mental, physical or spiritual.

Your objective mind and will are so vacillating that you usually only WISH for things and the wonderful, capable power within you does not function.

Most wishes are simply vocal expressions. Jimmy, the office boy, gave no thought of possessing the red roadster. Landem, the salesman, was not thinking of any other job or even thinking at all. President Bondum knew he had hay fever and was expecting it. Father's business was quite likely successful, and mother no doubt brought home first prize from the Bridge party that day, but they had no fixed idea of what they really wanted their children to accomplish and were actually helping to bring about the unhappy conditions which existed.

If you are in earnest about changing your present condition, here is a *concise, definite, resultful plan, with rules, explanations and suggestions.*

THE PLAN

WRITE down on paper in order of their importance the things and conditions you really want. Do not be afraid of wanting too much. Go the limit in writing down your wants. Change the list daily, adding to or taking from it, until you have it about right. Do not be discouraged on account of changes, as this is natural. There will always be changes and additions with accomplishments and increasing desires.

THREE POSITIVE RULES OF ACCOMPLISHMENT

1. *Read the list of what you want three times each day: morning, noon and night.*

2. *Think of what you want as often as possible.*

3. *Do not talk to any one about your plan except to the Great Power within you which will unfold to your Objective Mind the method of accomplishment.*

It is obvious that you cannot acquire faith at the start. Some of your desires, from all practical reasoning, may seem positively unattainable, but, nevertheless, write them down on your list in their proper place of importance to you.

There is no need to analyze how this Power within you is going to accomplish your desires. Such a procedure is as unnecessary as trying to figure out why a grain of corn placed in fertile soil shoots up a green stalk, blossoms and produces an ear of corn containing hundreds of grains, each capable of doing what the one grain did. If you will follow this definite plan and carry out the three simple rules, the method of accomplishment will unfold quite as mysteriously as the ear of corn appears on the stalk, and in most cases much sooner than you expect.

When new desires, deserving position at or about the top of your list, come to you, then you may rest assured you are progressing correctly.

It Works

Removing from your list items which at first you thought you wanted, *is another sure indication of progress.*

It is natural to be skeptical and have doubts, distrust and questionings, but when these thoughts arise, get out your list. Read it over; or if you have it memorized, talk to your inner self about your desires until the doubts that interfere with your progress are gone. *Remember, nothing can prevent your having that which you earnestly desire.* Others have these things. Why not you?

The Omnipotent Power within you does not enter into any controversial argument. *It is waiting and willing to serve when you are ready*, but your objective mind is so susceptible to suggestion that it is almost impossible to make any satisfactory progress when surrounded by skeptics. Therefore, choose your friends carefully and associate with people who now have some of the things you really want, but *do not discuss your method of accomplishment with them.*

Put down on your list of wants such material things as money, home, automobile, or whatever it may be, but do not stop there. Be more definite. If you want an automobile, decide *what kind, style, price, color,* and all the other details, including *when* you want it. If you want a home, plan the structure, grounds and furnishings. Decide on location and cost. If you want money, write down the amount, If you want to break a record in your business, put it down. It may be a sales record. If so, write out the total, the date required, then the number of items you must sell to make it, also list your prospects and put after each name the sum expected. This may seem very foolish at first, but you can never realize your desires if you do not *know positively and in detail what you want and when you want it.* If you cannot decide this, you are not in earnest. You must be definite, and when you are, results will be surprising and almost unbelievable. A natural and ancient enemy will no doubt appear when you get your first taste of accomplishment. This enemy is Discredit, in form of such thoughts as: "It can't be possible; it just happened to be. What a remarkable coincidence!"

When such thoughts occur *give thanks and assert credit to your Omnipotent Power* for the accomplishment. By doing this, you gain assurance and more accomplishment, and in time, prove to yourself that *there is a law, which actually works—at all times—* when you are in tune with it.

Sincere and earnest thanks cannot be given without gratitude and it is impossible to be thankful and grateful without being happy. Therefore, when you are thanking your greatest and best friend, *your Omnipotent Power*, for the gifts received, do so *with all your soul, and let it be reflected in your face.* The Power and what it does is beyond understanding. Do not try to understand it, but *accept the accomplishment* with thankfulness, happiness, and strengthened faith.

CAUTION

It is possible to want and obtain that which will make you miserable; that which will wreck the happiness of others; that which will cause sickness and death; that which will rob you of eternal life. You can have what you want, but you must take all that goes with it:

It Works

so in planning your wants, *plan that which you are sure will give to you and your fellow man the greatest good here on earth; thus paving the way to that future hope beyond the pale of human understanding.*

This method of securing what you want applies to everything you are capable of desiring and the scope being so great, it is suggested that your first list consist of only those things with which you are quite familiar, such as an amount of money or accomplishment, or the possession of material things. Such desires as these are more easily and quickly obtained than the discontinuance of fixed habits, the welfare of others, and the healing of mental or bodily ills.

It Works

Accomplish the lesser things first. Then take the next step, and when that is accomplished, you will seek the higher and really important objectives in life, but long before you reach this stage of your progress, many worthwhile desires will find their place on your list. One will be to help others as you have been helped. *Great is the reward to those who help and give without thought of self, as it is impossible to be unselfish without gain.*

It Works

IN CONCLUSION

A short while ago, Dr. Emile Coué came to this country and showed thousands of people how to help themselves. Thousands of others spoofed at the idea, refused his assistance and are today where they were before his visit.

So with the statements and plan presented to you now. You can reject or accept. You can remain as you are or *have anything you want.* The choice is yours, but God grant that you may find in this short volume the inspiration to choose aright, follow the plan and thereby obtain, as so many others have, all things, whatever they may be, that you desire.

(see next page)

It Works

Read the entire book over again, *and again*, AND THEN AGAIN.

Memorize the three simple rules on pages 15 and 16.

Test them now on what you want most *this minute.*

This book could have extended easily over 350 pages, but it has been deliberately shortened to make it easy as possible for you to read, understand and use. Will you try it? Thousands of bettered lives will testify to the fact that *"It Works."*

A Letter to You from the Author

Dear Reader:

The great possessions of life are all GIFTS mysteriously bestowed: sight, hearing, aspiration, love or life itself.

The same is true of ideas—the richest of them are given to us, as for instance, the powerful idea which this book has given you. What are you going to do with it? Are you surprised when I tell you the most profitable thing you can do is to give it away?

You can do this in an easy and practical way by having this book sent to those you know who NEED IT. In this way, you can help in the distribution of this worthwhile effort to make the lives of others better and happier.

You know people who are standing still or who are worried and discouraged. This is your chance to HELP THEM HELP THEMSELVES. If you withhold this book from them you will lose the conscious satisfaction that comes from doing good. If you see that they get this book, then you put yourself in line with the Law of Life which says, "You get by giving," and you may rightly expect prosperity and achievement.

At the very least you will have the inner sense of having done a good deed with no hope of being openly thanked and your reward will come secretly in added power and larger life.

THE AUTHOR

CPSIA information can be obtained
at www.ICGtesting.com
Printed in the USA
JSHW060203230722
28305JS00004BA/5